Planet
Earth

EARLY LIFE
ON EARTH

WAYLAND

www.waylandbooks.co.uk

First published in 2016 by Wayland
© Wayland 2016

Written by Michael Bright
Cover illustration by Mark Turner

Editor: Corinne Lucas
Designer: Grant Kempster

ISBN: 978 0 7502 9982 4

10 9 8 7 6 5 4 3 2 1

MIX
Paper from
responsible sources
FSC® C104740
www.fsc.org

Wayland

An imprint of

Hachette Children's Group

Part of Hodder & Stoughton

Carmelite House

50 Victoria Embankment

London, EC4Y 0DZ

An Hachette UK Company

www.hachette.co.uk

www.hachettechildrens.co.uk

Printed in China

contents

ORIGINS
of life

Shortly after the formation of Earth 4.6 *billion* years ago, liquid water was thought to have collected on our planet's surface and life may have appeared as early as four billion years ago. However, despite this kind of scientific guesswork, the origins of life are covered in mystery, for exactly when, where and how it happened is far from clear…

from chemicals to cells

The basic chemicals of life either 'dropped' on to Earth on *meteorites* from space or they were 'created' here. Lightning, ultraviolet light from the Sun, or heat from inside Earth changed them over time to make more complex chemicals. This was 'chemical *evolution*', and those chemicals were the forerunners of life's *molecules*. At some point they made copies of themselves and also gathered together to form cells, and each cell was surrounded by a wall. The cell was also able to copy itself, and so life began. This was the start of 'biological evolution'.

The landscape of early Earth.

INVASION FROM SPACE

Life may not have started on Earth. Some of the complex chemicals that make up living things have been found all over the Universe, so it is possible that life developed in any place where the conditions were right, including on our neighbour, Mars. Tiny living things then arrived on Earth as well-protected survival capsules called *spores*. They came to Earth on asteroids, comets or meteorites. Scientists call this theory *panspermia*.

cauldrons of life

Where life started is another mystery. Here are just a few places on Earth where it might have begun.

In hot springs, volcanic pools and *geysers*, which are heated by *molten* rock below the Earth's surface.

In deep-sea vents or *fissures* on the floor of the deep sea, which squirt out very hot water and *minerals*. They are known as hydrothermal vents.

The early ocean was a *primordial soup* that contained some of the ingredients for life. Energy from lightning or ultraviolet light from the Sun could have turned those chemicals into more complex ones that eventually led to living things.

FIRST LIFE

The first living things were probably very simple, single cells. They would have been similar to *bacteria*-like *organisms* that are alive today. They are found in hot springs and deep-sea vents, the sorts of places where life might have started.

survival of the fittest

After the first cells had established themselves, new life forms began to appear on Earth. They had gained an advantage over previous cells, because they could live in extreme conditions like those found on the early Earth. This made them slightly better and more able to survive. Scientists call this process evolution.

Archaea look like bacteria but are different.

Blue-green algae sometimes form lines or 'filaments'.

blue-green bacteria

The earliest life forms fed on chemicals in their environment, but then a life form appeared that could make its own food using the gas carbon dioxide. This gas was found in the *atmosphere*, water and the energy from sunlight. This food-process is called *photosynthesis*, and some of the first organisms to use it were blue-green algae, a type of bacterium that still exists today.

A fossil stromatolite made by ancient blue-green algae.

earliest signs of life

There are *traces* of life in *crystals* four billion years old, but the oldest recognisable forms of life are 3.48 billion years old and were found in Western Australia. They resemble the modern stromatolites, which look like cushion-shaped mats and are found in warm, shallow bays in Western Australia.

GEOLOGICAL TIME

Scientists divide the 4.6 billion years since Earth formed up to the present day into geological eons, eras, periods, epochs and ages. This table shows the main ones. Figures are in millions of years, except for the Holocene.

Eon	Era	Period	Epoch
Phanerozoic (541 to present)	Cenozoic (65.5 to present)	Quaternary (2.588 to present)	
			Holocene (11,700 years to present) Pleistocene 2.58 mya to 11,700 years)
		Neogene (23.03 to 2.58)	Pliocene (5.333 to 2.58) Miocene (23.03 to 5.333)
		Palaeogene (66 to 23.03)	Oligocene (33.9 to 23.03) Eocene (56 to 33.9) Palaeocene (66 to 56)
	Mesozoic (251 to 65.5)	Cretaceous (145 to 66)	
		Jurassic (201.3 to 145)	
		Triassic (252.17 to 201.3)	
	Palaeozoic (541 to 251)	Permian (298.9 to 252.17)	
		Carboniferous (358.9 to 298.9)	
		Devonian (419.2 to 358.9)	
		Silurian (443.8 to 419.2)	
		Ordovician (485.4 to 443.8)	
		Cambrian (541 to 485.4)	
Precambrian (4600 to 541)	Proterozoic (2500 to 541)		Ediacaran (635 to 541)
	Archean (4000 to 2500)		
	Hadean (4600 to 4000)		

first ANIMALS

Scientists are cautious about describing the 'first animal' because fossils are rare and identifying them is difficult. Living things that probably evolved from single-celled into multi-celled organisms could have made an appearance 1.5 billion years ago.

great-great-great-great-great ... grandmother

The earliest multi-celled organism could have been a sphere of cells, similar in shape to the green alga Volvox. From this, flatter creatures evolved with a top and bottom. They had at least two layers of cells and were similar to the modern Trichoplax, a small, flattened but shapeless animal about one millimetre (0.039 in) across. These flat animals were possibly the *ancestors* of all animals, including us.

Modern Volvox colonies.

first jellies

While sponges have traditionally been thought of as one of the first groups of animals to evolve, there is evidence to suggest that comb jellies may have beaten them to it. These would have been quite complex creatures, with a *nervous system*, unlike the sponges that have no nerves.

A comb jelly.

animals like plants

Hundreds of types of animals suddenly appeared during the Ediacaran period (635-541 million years ago or mya). Scientists call it the 'Avalon Explosion'. Most of the animals were soft-bodied and in the shape of discs, tubes or ferns and they stood or lay on the seabed.

One group was named the rangeomorphs. They were soft-bodied, fern-shaped creatures, up to 60 cm (24 in) high. They lived in the deep sea, where they took in food directly from seawater through the surface of their body. Few other creatures were gobbling up the food, so they had it all to themselves.

Kimberella used its tube-like *proboscis* to feed on mats of bacteria.

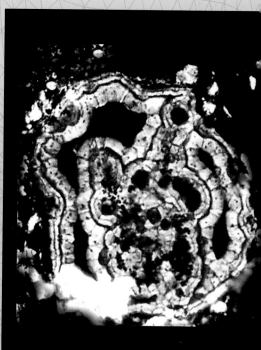

LEFT AND RIGHT

The first animal with a head and a left and right – known as bilateral symmetry – appeared during the Ediacaran period. It was worm-like and given the tongue-twisting name Vernanimalcula.

cambrian EXPLOSION

All the major groups of animals in the world today appeared during the Cambrian period (541-485.4 mya). It was a time when animals began to develop weapons and defences. It meant that some became *predators* and others their *prey*.

Anomalocaris had one of the first formidable weapons.

top predators

The most aggressive animal of this period was undoubtedly Anomalocaris. It was up to 2 m (6.6 ft) long and had a pair of arms, like shrimp tails, that grabbed its prey. On the underside of its head, its mouth had a ring of sharp teeth. Along its body were swimming flaps, so it must have been fast. It belonged to a group of animals know as *arthropods* and they are jointed-legged animals that include modern lobsters, insects and spiders.

Opabinia had lobes along its body and a fan-shaped tail.

tube sucker

One of the strangest creatures was Opabinia. It had a long, flexible proboscis, like a miniature elephant's trunk, but with grasping spines at its tip. Opabinia probably thrust this down burrows to grab any worms hiding inside. Its body was up to 8 cm (3 in) long. It might have been a *primitive* crustacean, related to shrimps and crabs, but then again maybe not.

Trilobites have three main body bits – head shield, body and tail shield.

The spines are covered with tiny triangular 'scales'.

spiky worms

Another oddball was Hallucigenia. It had tentacles with claws underneath its body for walking, and on its back were two rows of spines for protection. It was probably related to modern velvet worms: basically worms with legs.

TRILOBITES

These easy-to-recognise arthropods resembled modern woodlice or pill bugs. Some fed on the seabed, while others were free-swimming and fed on tiny living things floating in the water, called *plankton*. The biggest individuals reached 70 cm (28 in) in length during the Ordovician period (485.4-443.8 mya), and they were probably the most successful group of early animals. They existed for 270 million years, but they had died out by the end of the Permian period, about 252 mya.

armoured slug

Wiwaxia was an oval-shaped, slug-like animal with hard scales covering its sides and two rows of spines on its back. It was up to 5 cm (2 in) long and probably fed on mud on the seabed.

an age of
FISH

The first animals with backbones, or vertebrates, were fish. They appeared during the Cambrian period, about 530 mya, but the real giants did not rule the seas until the Devonian period, about 150 million years later.

Conodont teeth either grasp and crush prey or filtered the seawater.

Early fish-like Animals

The first fish-like creatures had a stiff rod called a notochord, rather than a backbone, running the length of their body. Some of the earliest were the conodonts. They were eel-like animals with hard cone- and comb-shaped teeth, large eyes, chevron-shaped muscles, fins with fin rays and a notochord. They were 1-40 cm (0.4-16 in) long, depending on the species.

first fish

Several fossil fish compete for the title of 'first fish', Pikaia being one of them. It was leaf-shaped, with a pair of head tentacles but no eyes, and resembled a modern lancelet. Its body was made up of rows of muscle blocks that pushed the animal along in S-shaped waves, like an eel.

Pikaia was 5 cm (2 in) long.

fish without jaws

Jawless, armoured fish had protective plates around their head. They had eyes, breathed with *gills*, and they fed by sucking prey into their jawless mouths. From one of these species evolved fish with jaws.

fish with jaws

The first fish with jaws and teeth were the placoderms. They were heavily armoured and most were predators. The largest known was Dunkleosteus, which lived about 360 mya. It was up to 11 m (36 ft) long, the length of a double-decker bus, and was thought to have been the world's first super-predator.

WATER MONSTERS

The early fish had to watch out for some of the largest arthropods that ever lived. They were sea scorpions known as euryptids, and the biggest type lived about 390 mya. It was 2.5 m (8 ft) long, with 46 cm (18 in) long claws. Sea scorpions were not true scorpions and many lived in fresh water, but they were one of the

INVASION
of the land

Life moved from the water onto the land in several stages. Carpets of algae were first, followed by simple plants. Close behind were insects and scorpions, and later came animals with backbones. Apart from everyday things, such as finding food and avoiding being eaten, the land presented new challenges. Animals had to get oxygen from the air rather than from water, and there was the risk of drying out.

first plants

About 450 years ago, during the Ordovician period, the first plants made it on to the land. They had evolved from green algae living in shallow freshwater pools that probably dried up each summer. Only fossil spores have been found, but they indicate these pioneering plants were similar to modern leaf-like liverworts. Most avoided drying out by living in dark, damp places.

A modern leaf-shaped liverwort.

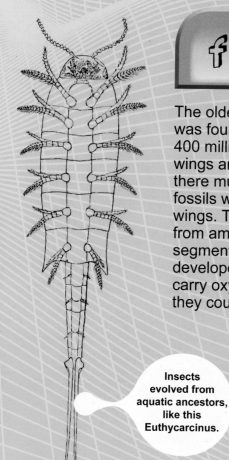

first insects

The oldest known insect fossil was found in Scotland and is 400 million years old. It had wings and was able to fly, so there must be even older insect fossils waiting to be found, without wings. They probably evolved from amphibious, hard-bodied, segmented creatures, and they developed a system of tubes to carry oxygen around the body so they could breathe in the air.

Insects evolved from aquatic ancestors, like this Euthycarcinus.

OLD FOUR LEGS

Coelacanths were lobe-finned fish that evolved about 425 mya, and surprisingly two species are still alive today, one in the western Indian Ocean and the other off Indonesia. They have changed very little in all that time, so are known as 'living fossils'.

Coelacanths have leg-like fins.

a leg on each corner

The lobe-finned fish were similar to modern lungfish. They gave rise to the first *amphibians* – animals with backbones that spend part of their life in water and part on land, such as frogs and salamanders.

Their fleshy fins turned into legs to walk on land, and their *swim bladders* evolved into lungs so they could breathe in the air.

An animal that shows this *transition* is Tiktaalik, which lived 375 mya during the Devonian period. Its shape was similar to a crocodile's, but it had fins like a fish.

385 mya

375 mya

365 mya

first SHARKS

About 450 mya, fish split into two main groups. One had a rigid bony skeleton, as in modern salmon, and the other had one made of bendy cartilage, as found in sharks and rays. Many of the early sharks had a streamlined, torpedo-shaped body, so they could swim fast. It seems sharks were successful ocean predators right from the start.

first shark-like fish

The spiny sharks lived at the beginning of the Silurian period (443.8-419.2 mya), but they were not like modern sharks. They had the same cartilage skeleton, but were covered with scales like modern gars and bowfins, which are bony fish.

few fossils

Sharks have left few clues about what they were like because their skeletons are made of soft, bendy cartilage. Most evidence comes from their teeth and tooth-like body scales. The earliest scales are 420 million years old and come from a shark called Elegestolepis. The earliest teeth are 400 million years old and from a Leonodus shark, but nobody knows what either looked like.

primitive shark

One of the earliest recognisable sharks was Cladoselache. It was 2 m (6.6 ft) long, streamlined, with stiff triangular fins. Fossilised fish remains found tail first in its stomach indicate it was a fast-swimming predator that could catch up with its prey. It lived about 370 mya.

Cladoselache had 5-7 gill slits.

freshwater sharks

The shark Xenacanthus lived in fresh water about 280 mya. It was an eel-shaped shark, about a metre (3.3 ft) long, with a very long spine on the back of its head. The dorsal fin on its back ran the length of its back and around its tail, like a modern conger eel.

GOLDEN AGE OF SHARKS

During the Carboniferous period, sharks and their relatives took on some bizarre shapes. The strangest must have been Helicoprion, which had a *whorl* of teeth in its lower jaws that resembled a circular saw. Another odd-ball was the Stethacanthus. Male sharks of this type had a shaving brush-like structure on their back, its function unknown.

GIANT
invertebrates

Jointed-legged animals, know as arthropods, grew to immense sizes during the Carboniferous and early Permian periods. One reason was that there were few large vertebrate predators to eat them up. Another was that there was a high level of oxygen in the atmosphere. Insects could take in more oxygen, so they could grow bigger.

giant dragonflies

About 300 mya, there were flying insects related to modern dragonflies that had wingspans up to 65 cm (25.6 in) across, the same as a wild duck. They were ferocious sky predators.

HOW DO WE KNOW?

What the very earliest life forms looked like is mainly guesswork, for they were made of soft parts that do not preserve well. For the rest, scientists rely on finding fossils in rocks. Fossils are whole plants and animals, or parts or traces of them, such as their footsteps or leaf prints, which have been preserved in rocks. When a living thing dies and *sediments* cover it, the chemicals in its body are replaced by minerals from the rock. It is literally turned to stone or, in the case of the swamp forests, into coal.

giant centipedes

Imagine a millipede 2.3 m (8.5 ft) long … yes, metres! This was the length of the plant-eating Arthropleura. Fossilised footprints, consisting of long, side-by-side rows of tiny footprints, show how this enormous millipede must have moved quickly through the forest. It was the world's largest known land invertebrate.

coal forests

The giant invertebrates lived in thick rainforests and swamp forests. The climate was tropical and the air moist. The trees grew tall, such as the 30 m (100 ft) high Lepidodendron, related to modern quillworts – small plants with long, thin hollow shafts for leaves. There were tree ferns and seed ferns, and a variety of low-growing plants. All of the trees and plants are thought to have pumped large amounts of oxygen into the air, up to 35 per cent, compared to 21 per cent today. Then, about 305 mya, the vegetation began to die down and sediments covered the remains. The plants were turned into coal.

Trees are buried in sediment before they decay.

Minerals replace the tree's tissues.

Soft rocks erode away leaving the stone fossil tree.

Trees die.

AMBHIBIANS
rule

For tens of millions of years, during the Carboniferous and early Permian periods, the dominant animals on Earth were amphibians. Some were small with thin, moist skin like today's frogs and salamanders, while others were big and very reptile-like monsters.

leaving the pond

One pre-amphibian four-legged vertebrate was called the Acanthostega. It was one of the first to have legs rather than fins, with fingers and toes. It couldn't walk too well so it probably waded through shallow swamps grabbing and eating invertebrate prey at the water's edge.

Two long bones supported Diplocaulus's head.

triangular head

Another pre-amphibian creature was the Diplocaulus. It had a salamander-shaped body, about a metre (3.3 ft) long and a large, boomerang-shaped head. This would have made it hard for predators to swallow, but would help it steer through water.

big head

One of the heaviest amphibians was the 3 m (10 ft) long Diadectes. It had a massive head, like a hippo, and was one of the first amphibians to be an exclusive plant-eater.

hide from the sun

The 3 m (10 ft) long Metoposaurus lived at a time when the climate alternated regularly between wet and dry. It survived the drought by digging a burrow with its broad, flat head and wide hands and hiding away. During the wet seasons, it hunted in lakes.

reptile-like amphibians

Many of the prehistoric amphibians had the shape of modern crocodiles. The Eogrinus was a slender beast, with scaly rather than moist skin. At 4.6 m (15 ft) long, it was one of the longer amphibians at the time. The Eryops was shorter at 2 m (6 ft) long, but sturdily built with massive, teeth-filled jaws and stocky, *splayed* legs.

MODERN AMPHIBIANS

The 20 cm (8 in) long Amphibamus is possibly the ancestor of all modern amphibians – frogs, toads, salamanders, newts and earthworm-like caecilians.

monster amphibians

Like all major predatory groups, the amphibians had their monsters. The Mastodonsaurus had a gigantic, flattened, crocodile-like head that took up the first third of its 6 m (20 ft) long body. It was one of the largest amphibians ever to have lived.

the first REPTILES

The earliest known reptiles lived in the rainforests during the late Carboniferous period, before the climate became drier. They were more suited to living on land than the amphibians. A key advance was the reptile egg. Amphibians laid their eggs in water, but reptile eggs contained water inside the egg so the baby reptile could develop safely on land.

reptile pioneer

One of the earliest known reptiles was the Hylonomus. It was a small, lizard-like animal about 20 cm (8 in) long that scampered about in the rainforest, avoiding the giant amphibians. It had tiny sharp teeth, and ate small insects.

Mesosaurus teeth turn outwards.

RETURN TO THE SEA

With giant amphibians disappearing, a few early reptiles returned to the water. The Mesosaurus had a metre (3.3 ft) long, streamlined body, webbed feet and propelled itself along with its long hind legs. It fed on shrimp-like creatures, and was probably a forerunner of the giant marine reptiles that later shared the planet with the dinosaurs.

all change

About 305 mya, many of the world's rainforests collapsed and dry conditions spread across much of the single supercontinent, Pangaea. Deserts were widespread, which favoured plants with seeds in a protective cover. The first modern trees – conifers, ginkgos and cycads – replaced many of the spore-producing plants, such as Lepidodendron. These conditions gave the reptiles an advantage. They began to take over the places where the amphibians had previously lived.

new predators

The mammal-like reptiles became the dominant predators on Earth. The 4.6 m (15 ft) long Dimetrodon is recognised by the enormous 'sail' on its back. Its function is unknown, but it might have helped control the animal's temperature. Dimetrodon looked like a dinosaur, but was not one. It was one of a group that gave rise to the reptiles that eventually became mammals.

The sail was more than a metre (3.3 ft) tall.

PREDATORS
vs prey

During the middle and late Permian period, several groups of very large reptile-like animals appeared. Some were big, stocky plant-eaters, and others were strong and formidable predators. The plant-eaters had heavy, thick skulls with bony bumps, and the predators had front teeth that interlocked.

giant predator

The meat-eating Titanophoneus had a massive skull with a long snout with interlocking front teeth. At up to 5 m (16 ft) long, it was one of the largest predators of its time, but its splayed legs indicate it was probably a bit slow. It ambushed its prey rather than running it down, killing its victim with a powerful bite to the neck.

Large canine teeth killed with a bite to the prey's neck.

heavy plant-eater

Tapinocephalus was a plant-eater with a huge barrel-shaped body and a massive bony roof to its skull, like a crash helmet. Males of the species probably engaged in head butting, like modern mountain sheep, to gain territory or a mate. Tapinocephalus was over 3 m (10 ft) long.

reptilian wolves

Lycosuchus and Pristerognathus were active predators that lived at the end of the Permian period, 265-245 mya. Both were about the size of a large dog, and Lycosuchus had two large canine teeth in each side of the upper jaw. Both beasts fed on small animals, perhaps hunting in packs like wolves.

EPIC BATTLES

Inostrancevia was part of a group of mammal-like reptiles that were *apex predators*, right at the top of their food chain. It was almost the size of a rhino, up to 3.5 m (11.5 ft) long, and had extra long canine teeth, which were 15 cm (6 in) long, like a sabre-toothed cat. It shared living space with the massive, plant-eating Scutosaurus. The *herbivore* was more than 3 m (10 ft) long and bulky, so it moved slowly. Its main defence was a skull sporting bony spikes and it had bony plates under its skin, like chain mail. No doubt predator and prey clashed often in the semi-deserts of the late Permian period.

Signs of the FUTURE

Towards the end of the Permian period, creatures were appearing that scientists recognise as the forerunners of modern animals, such as the mammals. They were reptilian, but they were beginning to show features that we would recognise today.

Standing tall

Bunostegos, meaning 'knobbly roof', was a cow-sized, plant-eating reptile with large bony knobs on and around its head. It was unusual in that it walked with its four limbs directly below its body, like a mammal, rather than splayed out to the side like a lizard. It was the first vertebrate with four legs to do so. It lived in a dry desert region in the centre of the Pangaea supercontinent, about 260 mya.

PERMIAN WILDLIFE

In the sea there were plenty of coral reefs around the coast of Pangaea. In deeper water, ammonites were common. Most had spiral shells, like a snail. Bony fish were replacing those lobe-finned fish that came before the amphibians. Bugs, similar to the ones we have today, started to appear on land. They had needle-like mouth parts to pierce plant stems and suck out the sap. Cicadas and beetles also arrived during the Permian period (289.9-252.17 mya).

 reptile mammals

The cynodonts, meaning 'dog teeth', were reptiles that were similar to mammals. The early species were relatively small and they appeared in the late Permian period. They had a second *palate* inside their mouth that allowed them to chew and breathe at the same time, speeding up digestion. Their predecessors swallowed everything whole without chewing. They had a large head like a mammal, but their brains were small. They were nudging towards being warm-blooded and the smaller cynodonts might have had fur and whiskers.

Procynosochus was an early cynodont.

The Procynosochus had teeth with a working surface like a mammal's cheek teeth. It might have had a diaphragm like we have as well. This is the flat muscle that separates the heart and lungs from the stomach and intestines. Procyonosochus probably chewed its food rather than just swallowing it, and it may have hunted in lakes and rivers.

Charassognathus was a fierce predator.

the time of the GREAT DYING

Life in the Permian period was brought to an abrupt end by the largest loss of plant and animal life in our planet's history. During this mass extinction, life on Earth almost disappeared completely. About 90 per cent of all species were wiped out, especially those living in the sea. Only 4 per cent survived and lived into the Triassic period (252.17-201.3 mya).

triple whammy

The cause of the mass extinction is unknown, but vast *lava fields* in northern Russia, known as the Siberian Traps, were probably involved in the mass extinction. They were formed by the largest volcanic eruptions in Earth's history, which lasted on and off for two million years. On top of that, it is likely that there was an impact from an asteroid. Scientists have found a 120 km (75 miles) wide crater of the right age in Australia. It was made by an asteroid 4.8 km (3 miles) across. It would have smothered the world in billions of tons of debris, dust, poisonous gases and *acid rain*. In addition, the oceans may have lost much of their oxygen at the time or turned acidic, making it difficult for life to survive. Altogether, these things made for a global catastrophe with very few survivors.

fungi heaven

Almost all of the world's trees disappeared during the mass extinction, but this was good news for fungi. The enormous quantities of dead wood meant the amount of fungi increased dramatically.

GREAT THINGS AHEAD

Amongst the survivors that made it through to the Triassic period were the archosaurs, meaning 'ruling reptiles', and their odd-shaped relatives, including the hippo-sized, parrot-beaked Hyperodapedon, and the ultra-slim, long-necked Prolacerta. Had the archosaurs not survived we would never have had the most famous group of prehistoric animals that ever lived … the dinosaurs.

triassic predators

The largest reptile to take over as apex predator after the mass extinction was the Erythrosochus. It had a stocky body, a large head on a short neck, and its powerful jaws were lined with sharp, conical-shaped teeth. Another large predator, which was similar to a modern-day crocodile, was the Proterosochus. It was probably an ambush predator that waited for animals to come to the water, much like a Nile crocodile.

29

glossary

acid rain   rain containing high levels of dangerous chemicals that turn the rain from neutral to acid

amphibian   an animals with a backbone that live partly in water and partly on land.

ancestor   an animal from which later animals evolved.

apex predator   a hunter at the top of the food chain.

arthropod   a hard-bodied, jointed-legged animal without a backbone.

atmosphere   the layer of gases around a planet.

bacteria   a group of single-celled living things, some of which cause diseases.

billion   a thousand million.

crystal   a see-through solid with a clear geometric shape and regular faces.

evolution   the gradual process by which something living changes into a better form.

fissure   a crack in rocks.

geyser   a natural hot spring that squirts boiling water into the air.

gills   organs used by fish for breathing underwater.

herbivore   an animal that eats plants.

lava field   a large area of hot, liquid (molten) volcanic rock that has cooled and become solid.

meteorite   a piece of rock or metal that has fallen onto Earth from space.

minerals   chemical not made by plants or animals, which have been formed by a geological process.

molecule   the smallest part of a substance that can take part in a chemical reaction.

molten   hot and liquid.

nervous system   the network of nerve cells and fibres that carries electrical impulses from one part of the body to another

organism   a living thing.

palate   the separation of the mouth and nose cavities in the roof of the mouth.

panspermia   the theory that life on Earth arose first somewhere in space.

photosynthesis   the process by which green plants, algae and blue-green algae create sugars using carbon dioxide, water and energy from the Sun.

plankton   tiny living things that float about in the sea.

predator   an animal that hunts and eats other animals.

prey   an animal that is eaten by another animal.

primitive   the early stage of something.

primordial soup   the name given to Earth's early ocean because it contained many of the ingredients needed to make life, much like a soup.

proboscis   nose-like structure

sediments   tiny particles of rock that are carried by wind, water or ice.

splayed   spread out to the sides.

spore   a seed-like form that a bacterium changes into so it can withstand bad conditions.

swim bladder   an air-filled sac inside a fish that helps it stay at the right depth in the water.

trace   tiny amount.

transition   a change from one thing to another.

whorl   a coiled shape.

further information

Books

Life on Earth: The Story of Evolution (2002)
Steve Jenkins
Houghton Mifflin Harcourt
ISBN-13: 978-0618164769

The Complete Guide to Prehistoric Life (2005)
Tim Haines and Paul Chamber
BBC Books
ISBN-13: 978-0563522195

Websites

Animals of the Burgess Shale
http://www.burgess-shale.bc.ca

History of Life on Earth
http://www.bbc.co.uk/nature/history_of_the_earth

How some of the first animals lived – or died
http://www.cam.ac.uk/research/news/how-some-of-the-first-animals-lived-and-died

DVDs

David Attenborough's First Life (2010)
BBC DVD

Lost World, Vanished Lives (2012)
BBC Earth DVD

titles in the series

THE BIG BANG AND BEYOND

MICHAEL BRIGHT

Origin of the Universe
The Sun
Origins of the Solar System
Origins of Earth
Origin of the Moon
Onion skin Earth
Dynamic Earth
Earth's early atmospheres
Lightning strike
Climate change
Earth's water
Blue planet
Habitable planet
Glossary
Index
Further information

ISBN: 9780750296670

EARLY LIFE ON EARTH

MICHAEL BRIGHT

Origins of life
First life
First animals
Cambrian explosion
An age of fish
Invasion of the land
First sharks
Giant invertebrates
Amphibians rule
The first reptiles
Predators vs prey
Signs of the future
The time of the great dying
Glossary
Index
Further information

ISBN: 9780750299824

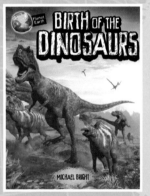

BIRTH OF THE DINOSAURS

MICHAEL BRIGHT

The survivors
The first dinosaurs
The meat-eaters
Monster predators
Feathered dinosaurs
Giant plant-eaters
Duckbills
Crash helmets and spikes
Armoured dinosaurs
Undersea hunters
Flying reptiles
Demise of the dinosaurs
Birth of the birds
Glossary
Index
Further information

ISBN: 9780750296687

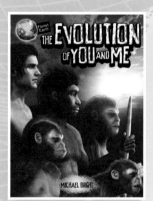

THE EVOLUTION OF YOU AND ME

MICHAEL BRIGHT

Time of opportunity
The birds are coming!
Hot and cold Earth
Ancient and modern
Planet of the apes
A time for whales
Early walkers
Southern ape-men and relatives
Early humans
Neanderthals and hobbits
Modern humans
Kingdom of the horse
The humans are coming!
Glossary
Index
Further information

ISBN: 9780750296694

PEOPLE AND PLANET EARTH

MICHAEL BRIGHT

Stone Age
First farmers
Taming wild animals
Villages and towns
Metals and knowledge
World explorers
Age of enlightenment
Age of machines
Getting about
Black gold
Pollution alert
Winds of change
A future for planet Earth
Glossary
Index
Further information

ISBN: 9780750296700

JOURNEY INTO SPACE

MICHAEL BRIGHT

The space race
Manned space flight
Space stations
Observing the edge of the Universe
Close to the Sun
The red planet
King of the planets
Jewel in the Solar System
The ice-giants
Comets
Asteroids
Pluto and beyond
The final frontier
Glossary
Index
Further information

ISBN: 9780750298292